ner

Cancer & Bling

PROJECT Y PUBLISHING

First published in Great Britain in 2017 by Project Y Publishing

A CIP catalogue record for this book is available from the British Library

ISBN 978-1-78745-063-9

CANCER & BLING

This book is dedicated to my mum, whom I love and adore, and whose memory will remain in my heart for eternity.

CHAPTER 1

On the 18th January 1996, I gave birth to our beautiful baby son Marc, weighing in at 7lb, 3oz. He had huge hazel eyes - just like his father's - and hardly any hair. Marc was a miracle, not because we were told that we couldn't have children, but because he was so perfect and we had made him. It was an incredulous feeling to have created our own perfect baby boy.

I had wanted a normal birth, with an epidural (of course), but ended up being induced as everything had started to swell, including my fingers and ankles. So it was uncomfortable to walk or even to lie in bed. While I was laying in the delivery suite waiting for some thing to happen, Russell, my darling husband, was on his mobile and laptop, at the same time, doing deals.

Russell was a motivated self-made entrepreneur, who worked at a hundred miles an hour and was very astute in business. The nurse, who had been monitoring me, came in and scolded Russell, telling him to turn it all off. My blood pressure had shot up and was dangerously high.

The gynaecologist was called and immediately recommended that I have an emergency Caesarean Section, for the safety of our baby and myself. Russell was gowned-up in an instant and a small screen was placed on top of my bulbous tummy.

I was given a running commentary by my husband, whose head was turning from left to right (like watching a tennis match), telling me what he could see. With little or no pain, thanks to the epidural, our gorgeous baby boy was delivered, wrapped in a towel, and put on my chest. I remember crying in disbelief, and I was not only very emotional but felt ecstatic at the same time.

"Do you have a name for him?" asked Angus, our gynaecologist.

"Yes, Marc Roland" Russell answered, straight away. We had only had girl's names and could not think of a boy's name that we liked, but deep down I had always loved the name Marc spelt with a 'c'.

Roland was Russell's father's name; he had tragically been killed in a car accident at the age of fifty. He left his wife Coralie a widow at the age of forty, with three young boys to bring up on her own - Russell was just sixteen and his two younger brothers, thirteen and eleven, were catastrophically left without a father. In effect, Russell, being the eldest, was father figure to his two younger brothers. He had to grow up extremely quickly, and was very determined, unswayable and very much a businessman.

I had always told Russell I wanted twelve dozen red roses upon the birth of our baby, as my Dad had showered my mum with red roses on my birth. Sure enough, when Russell returned to my room, the scented perfume from the roses was unbelievable, as well as the sight of so many vases with over 144 red roses.

This was amazing and brought tears to my eyes. I had only been joking as I didn't expect so many, but it was so, so lovely. As I was lying there, looking at our gorgeous creation, my mum, dad and mother-in-law Coralie, all turned up with huge blue teddy bears, cellophane on platters, baby accessories and cards.

Friends and family descended on us all the time to welcome our next generation baby boy. Very soon my room was adorned with flowers, cards, bears, toys and outfits, in fact so much so that the hospital ran out of vases. It was such a special time welcoming our son Marc, after nine long months of cooking him.

Being a career woman, it was a life changing experience to become a mum, but totally wonderful to have created another generation. Some three or four months later, still getting used to motherhood and sharing getting up throughout the night, I wanted to get my brain back into gear. So I returned to work as sales manager of a busy Contract IT recruitment company. A full-time Nanny looked after our little Prince. It felt like I had a limb missing as I missed Marc so much that I kept phoning home to see how he was.

I became so busy mentally and physically that I barely took any notice of a small lump appearing on my right breast, and, indeed, only felt it when lifting my double D breast into my bra. My Mum Hilary, who worked full time with my Dad Maurice in their family luggage business, was disturbed when I mentioned this in passing. She immediately insisted I make an appointment with our doctor.

I really didn't want to be bothered as I was back in the swing of things, working, travelling and being a mum. Geminis always do more than one thing at a time, always multi-tasking. Eventually, after much nagging by Mum and Russell, I gave in and went to see our GP.

On examining me, he said: "Well, this is just a milk gland, here are some tablets. Come back and see me in a couple of weeks if it does not go away". So off I trotted, placating everyone's fears of the worst, and started taking my tablets.

Some three weeks later, the lump had not gone, indeed it was more obvious to the touch. Yet still, I was dismissive, claiming I was too busy and it was probably nothing. Eventually, I was cajoled into making another appointment to see my GP.

I called, only to be told he had gone on holiday for three weeks, and I was asked if I wanted to see someone else? Mum and Dad insisted that I see a specialist, as did Russell and Coralie, my mother-in-law.

Not knowing who to go to, I returned to my Gynaecologist for his opinion.

"Lisa" he said, "whatever it is, good or bad, it should not be there. So I'm going to recommend you to the top breast specialist I know in Harley Street".

My heart skipped a beat. Having ignoring this lump in my breast, could it be cancer? Or was it a nodule? Fear started to creep in as I anticipated the worst.

This was the start of my life changing completely. Something that would turn my world completely upside down, that ultimately gave me abnormal strength, willpower, determination and a tenacious fight for survival. It's the inspiration of living through this, both physically and mentally, that I want to share with you. It may inspire you, or someone you know going through this horrid disease, to learn to cope and, indeed, to survive.

Cancer is probably the most frightening of all diseases as you don't know what to expect, or if you can survive. So you live each day on an emotional roller coaster, not knowing what tomorrow may bring.

I want to share with you how I coped with catastrophic diagnoses, with the immeasurable support of my family and friends who were there for me throughout.

How each time doctors gave me death sentences, or told me that I shouldn't be here based on the most aggressive tumours that I had, and how I ultimately survived and am still here. I was never in remission as I was always at high risk of relapse. My son and family were my burning fire to get through it all repeatedly.

How this changed my perspective on life and how I can help you, or someone you know, to live and survive.

CHAPTER 2

The following day, I went to Harley Street with Russell. We were ushered into a very regal waiting room with a table in the centre covered with glossy magazines and newspapers. Paintings and caricatures depicted amusing medical situations with humorous anecdotes.

After we had studied our surroundings for some time, a nurse walked in and called my name. We hurriedly rose from our seats and were ushered into an enormous office, more like a grand hall. Sitting behind a large antique rosewood desk in a huge leather studded chair, was Jerry the breast surgeon. He rose from his chair, to his full six foot two height and twenty stone frame, as we gingerly entered.

"Please sit down" he said, in a deep, commanding voice.

We watched as he read the referral letter, which had been faxed to him by our gynaecologist.

"OK, let's have you up on the couch and see what we have. Just remove your upper clothes, and I will be with you in a moment." He closed a cream linen curtain around the bed while I undressed.

To my embarrassment, the curtain was suddenly pulled back, and he asked me to sit on the bed facing him. He felt the area, just above my nipple, and said:

"Right, I'm going to do a biopsy."

"What's that?" I asked.

"It's a needle aspiration".

"Right now?" I said, surprised.

"Yes, just close your eyes, this won't take a minute".

With his burly frame and strong authoritarian voice, I obeyed Suddenly I felt a sharp pain in my breast.

"Ow, that really hurts," I yelled.

"It's over now, you can get dressed," he said.

Once again I did as I was told. Returning to the desk, we asked what would happen next.

"I will have my lab report on this. Please advise the girls on reception on your way out that you will return in an hour."

"OK, thank you," we said.

We walked out quite numb. Russell tried to reassure me that everything would be ok and that the breast surgeon appeared to be very thorough. An hour felt like an eternity, but, eventually, we returned.

"My doctor told me it was probably a milk gland," I said meekly.

"Your doctor does not know what he is talking about."

Our hearts sank.

"The report showed an abnormality. We will need to operate tomorrow morning and will make arrangements at the Princess Grace Hospital. We will only excise the cell. I will have my pathologist on hand to tell me what it is and we'll go from there. We won't remove your breast, so don't worry."

Don't worry? What were we supposed to do? Of course we were worried; we felt sick and panic stricken. We walked out in a dazed state, with so many questions in our heads, not able to digest this mammoth information.

There was no history of cancer in my family, so why had this happened? How did it happen? Had I done something terrible for this to happen? Could it be that dreaded word.... cancer?

We phoned home and relayed the information to my parents' sinking hearts.

"We don't know anything yet, except it has to be removed," I said, trying to sound upbeat, but failing miserably.

Russell and I didn't know what to say to one another on the journey home. So we decided I should start to make a list of questions that I needed to answer, before signing any consent forms.

That evening was a blank to us both, we were completely dazed.

Russell's mum said: "face the problem if and when it happens".

She was right, but somehow, deep down, I knew something was wrong. 'Keep positive' was another phrase everyone kept saying to me. If I had a pound for every time I heard that, I would have been a millionaire. I grew to hate people saying this all the time. In reality, I had just been trying to ignore the lump and had hoped it would go away, but it hadn't.

We woke early next morning to travel to London. So much traffic, I just wanted to get there and get it over and done with. Finally, we arrived at the hospital and parked outside. My heart was pounding as we were ushered to my room. It was very pleasant, yet still it was not a hotel, it was a hospital. The seriousness of what was about to happen in these clinical surroundings suddenly hit me.

We saw the anaesthetist and my breast surgeon, who told me that forty minutes after I returned from the recovery area, I would know the results of the surgery. Jerry, the surgeon, would have his pathologist on hand to advise him.

While being wheeled down on a bed, I watched the gaps between the ceiling lights, until I arrived into the Pre-Med room to be put to sleep. I remember my heart pounding while counting back from ten to zero, but don't recall anything after seven.

"Lisa, have you got any pain, are you awake?" a nurse asked.

I was so tired and just wanted to keep my eyes closed and sleep, but instead I nodded to acknowledge being awake. Finally, I left the recovery room and returned to my own room, where Russell was waiting for me.

I felt so woozy and sleepy, and it was so hard to keep my eyes open. Eventually I managed to wake up properly, and at forty minutes to the second after returning to my room, the huge wooden door swung open, and in walked my giant of a surgeon, still robed in his green surgical gown.

Pulling down his mask (which I will never forget), he said: "Well Lisa, you are a very lucky woman, another two weeks and you would have been dead. You had a most aggressive cancerous tumour - which would have killed you - we caught it just in time. I have removed the tumour, but we're going to do one more operation tomorrow morning to leave a wide area excision around the site. Then we'll talk about what happens next. Have you any questions?"

We were dumbfounded and shook our heads.

"Ok then, see you tomorrow pre-surgery," he said, and walked out.

We were both totally speechless and astounded. Had we heard that correctly or was it a dream? Tears rolled down my cheeks. I had only just had our baby, the happiest moment of my life, but here I was lying in a hospital bed, age 31, and being told I had cancer. Had they got all of it? What would happen next? Would I live to see my son grow up? How could we be so happy one minute and so distraught the next? Why had it happened?

Next morning, I was wheeled back down to the theatre, and they removed a further amount of tissue that had surrounded the tumour to make sure they hadn't left anything. From being very embarrassed about my body, I lost all my inhibitions and I didn't care what they did to me, so long as they got rid of it all.

Following this, I saw my breast surgeon again, and he told me I would need to see an oncologist to have chemotherapy and radiotherapy – 'belt and braces' as they call it. Clearly he didn't want to take any chances, and I just wanted to live to see our son grow up.

Back in my room, the following day, I put makeup on, and did my hair. Russell, family and friends were amazed at how I looked as were all the medical staff, who nearly fell into the room on seeing me, their patient, looking so glamorous. They couldn't believe what I had just been through from the way I looked.

I just felt that if I looked terrible I'd feel even worse, and people would treat me differently by being over sympathetic when I just wanted to get back to normal. So by looking like me with my makeup and hair done, I felt psychologically a hundred times better.

On discharge, I was recommended to a professor of oncology, who was local to me and absolutely wonderful. Neville was very experienced, up on the latest research, and used all the latest technology that research could develop. Whatever he suggested had been thought through thoroughly. I felt lucky to have such an experienced team, but I was extremely tearful when friends or even strangers asked me about it. Then I thought: pull yourself together Lisa, they've caught it in time, and I just have to get on with it. So, after a few weeks, I went back to work, worked during the week, had intravenous chemotherapy on a Friday morning, felt sick for two to three days, and then returned to work the following week. Once again, everyone could not believe what I was going through, as I looked just the same – fully made up and immaculately dressed.

I was tired, sick and in pain, but so determined not to let it get to me that often people forgot what I was going through. I just don't know where this inner strength came from, but I felt that if I gave into it and became reclusive, I wouldn't get through it, and at no time did I want to feel like a cancer patient.

I often glanced at myself as I walked past a mirror with my hair and makeup done, and I felt like me. Yes, the chemo side effects made me sick, and the muscle spasms were awful, but I just had to be there for Marc and Russell, my family, friends and all who supported me.

I was going to live on, come what may. Everyone told me I was so brave and positive. Yet I did not feel brave at all, I just knew that I had to fight like a boxer to survive and beat cancer. I had to see my son grow up.

CHAPTER 3

Before starting chemo, I was told I would lose my hair. My hair was my crowning glory and was always immaculately set in place. Losing it would show the world that I was a cancer patient, and I did not want the attention to lure sympathy, I just wanted to look like me.

Looking back, this was actually the worst part of the treatment as waking each morning, I would see more and more hair on my pillow. I cried and cried, and finally plucked up the courage to buy a wig. I was so emotional and somewhat embarrassed when trying on so many, and then I finally found a style that was longer than my own hair. It was actually made by Dolly Parton and resembled my own big and bouncy blonde hair. I was advised to buy two wigs so when one needed washing, I could wear the other. They were so nice in the shop and so understanding, even when I burst into tears. They told me to buy a different colour in the same style for variety, so that it looked like I had had it highlighted. I bought a blonde one and a highlighted blonde one, and at the same time I had to buy a kit of wig shampoo, conditioner, a special wig brush and a couple of turbans to wear when at home. When I had done this, I finally came to the conclusion that it was inevitable, and decided to have my crowning glory all cut off.

Tears streamed down my face as Glenda, my hairdresser, cut all my hair off until all I could see was my scalp. To lose my hair was the most awful thing as it was blonde and always in place. I could not bring myself to look in mirror without it. Losing my hair was worse than the treatment, so I would advise anyone reading this not to prolong the agony. If you know you are going to lose your hair, don't wait, and have it all off as soon as possible. It's better to do this than see your hair shedding all the time on your pillow, in your brush, or just by running your fingers through it. I always wore a turban at home, or my wig when seeing any friends or going out.

As well as my hair, my eyebrows, eyelashes and body hair fell out too. It was great for a leg wax, but that was the only benefit. So everything ended up being glued on, stuck on or drawn on so I could look normal.

Normality is all that I wanted, and my darling Russell always told me how beautiful I was. I suggested we make an optician's appointment for him. Marc was only a baby, so he didn't know anything about his Mummy looking so different. Once I started to wear my wigs every day, I began to feel like me again, and in reality they were worth every penny as I didn't want to walk around bald headed and have pitying looks from strangers.

Indeed, I remember walking into a shop, wearing my wig for the first time and being very self-conscious when a sales assistant remarked on how beautiful my hair looked. That was, without a doubt, a definite confidence boost. It clearly didn't look like a wig as she thought it was my own hair.

There were six months of the most gruelling chemotherapy, when I was hooked up to an intravenous line and given a cocktail of drugs, from steroids, anti-sickness, piriton (which made me very sleepy as soon as it went through the line), and the chemo. I ended up having the most awful side effects. I felt nauseous so I took anti-sickness pills, which then gave me constipation followed by haemorrhoids. So it was a vicious circle.

On top of that, I experienced severe muscle spasms as a result of nerve endings being attacked by the toxic chemotherapy drugs in my body. I learnt that the side effects of the treatment would become more aggressive as the treatment progressed, as it was cumulative.

I was given a break before commencing radiotherapy. As my parents and my husband worked, my mother-in-law Coralie - an extrovert, non-stop chatterbox and ultra-positive lady - took it upon herself to take me to radiotherapy every day for a month.

She pulled me out of any depressing moments and spoke to me without pity or sympathy, which was what I really needed.

'Face a problem, if and when it happens,' became one of her sayings and when it did happen, she said: "Well, they haven't given you a sentence, have they? They are giving you treatment because they know it will help get rid of it, otherwise they wouldn't give it to you, would they?"

So true.

So many times friends broke down in front of me, which didn't help at all. Or they speak to me with that sympathetic voice as if I had died and gone to heaven. This doesn't help anyone going through this. You just want to be treated normally and not have your whole conversation consumed by this subject.

While the disease is internal with certain forms of cancer, it can be detected externally by weight loss or change of eye colour. This is what we saw at the North Middlesex hospital, where I had radiotherapy. Many fellow patients clearly had no future ahead of them, and it was, I have to say, so pitiful and depressing.

You didn't want to make it obvious that you were looking and that you knew the inevitable, yet somehow you did. I thought to myself, they are worse off than me and at least I haven't been given a life sentence. It seems terrible to say that other people's less fortunate circumstances in a strange way gave me the strength and encouragement to pick myself up and carry on fighting. I had not been given a sentence, and I was being given every chance to get over it.

The Radiotherapy that followed was not in itself painful; it was just the build-up, the fear, anticipation and tiresomeness of the treatment that affected me. Towards the end of twenty-five to thirty treatments, I became sunburnt under my breast and it was not conducive to wearing a bra, due to the skin being so sore and sensitive.

In time, this faded, and I could resume my normal life again, grateful after many scans that it had worked, and I'd come through the other side. I was for the first time a survivor, mentally and physically. I hadn't given in to it and had fought to get through it. My main motivation was to see our son grow up with both his parents. In reality, it was as much a mental fight as physical to get through the treatment.

At this time, it occurred to both Russell and I that I had been misdiagnosed by my GP, who was shortly about to retire. We contacted the medical council with a view to suing him, but they closed ranks and we could see we would not get anywhere.

Looking back twenty one years ago, I guess that GPs just did not see this type of thing as regularly as they do today. As a patient, realising I could have died from his misguided assessment, we wanted justice, but it was not to be. This was not the last time that I would be misdiagnosed either.

Our son Marc, a toddler now, was thankfully unaware of all my hospital visits, stays and treatments. To him, it was normal to see his Mummy going off to hospital and coming back more exhausted each day. He was into everything, and particularly loved his toy golf clubs and trolley, which his cousin Martin had bought him for his second birthday. He took them everywhere and never stopped playing with them. Ironically, we discovered this was to be his passion in life and indeed his future.

Our lives thankfully resumed some normality. I was scanned and had check-ups every three months, getting anxious before each appointment about what they might find and if anything would return. Thankfully, it was all clear after many scans and examinations. The bad news was that we were advised not to consider having any further children as if I became pregnant again, the chances were very high that the cancer would return. If it did, it would be virulent and incurable. It was, in effect, be here and be happy with one child or have more but don't survive.

It was extremely hard news to bear. If you, as a couple, elect not to have more children, then that's your given prerogative. But when you're told that you can't have more or you won't survive, the decision has been taken away from you. You feel cheated out of planning your future family. However, we were so happy to have our amazing son that we did not revisit this until later.

We decided to investigate adopting another child, but we were soon put off as all that we could be offered was a six, seven or eleven-year-old battered child, who would most likely have had major psychological issues.

The only baby we could be offered would be one of a different ethnic origin, who would not resemble us in any way. At this stage,

I considered how I might love an adopted baby in the same way as our own flesh and blood. Downhearted as we both were, we decided not to progress with this as we had been blessed with such a beautiful perfect baby and as we were so lucky to have a son. I was an only child and had not felt deprived of brothers or sisters. Indeed, I felt lucky not to have to share possessions, clothes or my parents love and adoration for me with anyone else.

As both Russell and I were ambitious and career orientated, we were used to travelling regularly on business, together wherever possible. My illness had made us closer than close, realising that I could have so easily died. Our precious little baby soon became a toddler, and we were so happy that all was well. We counted our blessings as my recovery from something so life threatening meant that we could be together again as a family.

CHAPTER 4

In January 1999, three years had elapsed, and the past was a distant memory filed somewhere in the back of our brains. We both felt normal again and were getting on with our lives.

While out walking one day, I suddenly felt an arresting pain in my ribs just below my right breast. As I bent over with this sharp, stabbing pain, I drew breath and wondered what on earth it could be. I forgot about it and continued as normal until it recurred a number of times, prompting me to see my oncologist.

Could it be my medication? Why had this happened now? What was it?

Neville, my oncologist, initially suggested that perhaps I had done it either at the gym or indeed lifted something too heavy and pulled a muscle. I told him that neither of the above were applicable as I had given up the gym and really didn't lift anything heavy. He could tell from my worried expression that I was panicking and so he said: "OK, I'll send you for a chest x-ray now, so we can be sure you're ok."

As he filled out the request form, I thought to myself, here we go again with another scan. All my scans had been routine so far, so I had no reason to think this would be any different. Perhaps I had pulled something internally? I had the x-ray and duly returned to see Neville, who was studying the x-rays for an inordinate amount of time. He was not happy, and my heart sank.

"I can see a shadow," he said, pointing to the x-ray on a backlit screen.

"Where is it?" I asked, starting to shake in shock.

"On the upper lobe of your lung. I want to run some further tests, a PET/CT scan and an MRI scan, to be sure."

My body went into shutdown; how could this be? I started trembling like a leaf whilst Russell held my hand.

"Let's get it investigated and not make our minds up until we know anything for sure," he said, trying to comfort me.

But deep down inside, we both somehow knew what it could be, and the past came flashing back. I needed to get the tests done straight away. I just had to know for definite what it was. What had a pain underneath my breast got anything to do with a shadow on my upper lung above my breast? Was it a coincidence, or could it have come back?

Multiple tests confirmed what I had been dreading the most: another recurrence of an abnormal cell. At this time, they could not be sure if it was a secondary one from my breast. Russell and I looked into each other's eyes, and I thought, oh no, how can we be here again? But somehow we were, and we just went through the motions mechanically, I suppose because we had been there before.

My Mum and Dad, my mother-in-law, and friends were all in total shock. Even before the removal of the tumour and a pathologist's report, I instinctively surmised it was cancer. Indeed, I had always believed that if you got lung cancer, you would not survive and almost certainly die. I had not been a smoker or a drinker. So why had this happened? 'Why?' is the number one question you ask yourself as the patient. It is because you are incredulous of something so serious, so life threatening, and you are looking for an explanation.

It's something you always think happens to someone else and not you. If we knew why, research would know how to cure the most dreaded disease of our century. There is no answer at this time, only suggestions: family history, smoking, drinking, food and so on. So it's a very hard pill to swallow.

It even made me consider if I had done something terrible, perhaps in a former life, to endure this agony all over again. Knowing what would follow, in many ways, made it harder. I knew what the side effects were but didn't bargain on how dangerous the operation was likely to be, and how difficult and long recuperation would take. Everyone was besides themselves with worry for my survival as lung cancer is so serious and life threatening.

We saw the lung surgeon at the London Independent hospital. He studied the x-ray and all my other scans.

"We have to remove it. I'll try to do it by keyhole surgery if I can as this will give you a far quicker recovery."

"If you can?" Russell said.

"Yes, if we can reach it. If not, we'll have to break open Lisa's ribcage and remove it, in which case the recovery will be lengthier."

This time we had a list of questions as to how long surgery would take, how soon I could have it done, how long I would be in hospital, when we would know if it was definitely cancer and so forth.

The lung surgeon was very patient and answered everything. Once again, I just wanted it over and done with as soon as possible. How quickly could he operate? In reality, I was not looking at the risk factor, only that I wanted it out of my body as quickly as possible, before it triggered off anything else.

What I didn't realise though, was how complex, lengthy and dangerous the operation was, even when I was signing the consent form. The only difference this time, was that somehow, deep down inside, I thought I might not come out of the operation. So I wrote a long letter to my husband, my son, my parents and my family to say goodbye. I hid the letter in my personal belongings, just in case, because no one really knows what could happen, do they? Looking back, this just seems so sad, but it was a necessary thing to do.

The operation took hours and hours, and part way through, the surgeon stopped the operation as he could not reach the tumour through keyhole surgery. He telephoned Russell to come in immediately as there was a complication. Russell rushed to the hospital with the operation on hold as he needed to sign another consent form for the surgeon to break open my ribcage. At that stage, he told Russell I had, at best, a 50/50 chance of survival. He signed the forms and surgery continued for many hours into the evening whilst Russell waited with my parents, not knowing whether I would come through the surgery. I can't begin to think what I put my family through mentally. This disease is not only physical but mental, both for the patient and their family and friends. They are utterly helpless as your life is totally in the hands of your medical team.

I remember waking up in intensive care, unaware of all the tubes, drips and drains, oxygen mask and everything around me. I saw Russell and my Mum and Dad at my bedside, not fully realising what could have happened.

"She's awake!" my Mum cried, with tears in her eyes.

I don't know what I said, as I tried to speak, but I was so pleased to see them all.

I had to have so much morphine for the pain, and my recuperation involved me blowing into a paper bag to re-inflate my lung. I had to relearn to breathe, eat and walk again. It was so debilitating and much like being reduced back to a baby state. I was unable to do anything for myself in the early days. But with each day that went by, I grew stronger and more determined.

I shocked my family and friends as when I came out of the High Dependency Unit and returned to my room, I was sitting up in bed with my hair done and my make-up on. It was my way of feeling normal. Even the doctors nearly fell into the room when they saw me. They wondered who this new glamorous patient was. I have always had a theory that if you look good, you feel good. It really helps and also stops people giving you pitying looks and feeling sorry for you. I just wanted to get back to normal, even though I had just had lung cancer surgery.

At this stage, I was not fit enough, physically or mentally, to return to work as I was told no stress. So I became a housewife, something I'd never been before. I had always worked from the moment I achieved my A levels, so to suddenly be forced to stop made me feel guilty. I would go out for lunches or coffees when I felt marginally up to it, but I felt I should be working.

Yet in reality, there was no way I could have worked, physically or mentally. I'd lost the upper lobe of my lung, and this in turn made me breathless from any type of exertion. I could not drive for some considerable time, so I was reliant on everyone chauffeuring me. I hated relying on people, especially as I was used to being so independent, but everyone was so kind and helpful.

Once again I had to have six courses of powerful chemotherapy and radical radiotherapy. I think this time round knowing what to expect actually made it harder as I was aware how these toxins could have severe painful side effects and cause extreme tiredness. More often than not, it's better to know the outline and not research all the information as the anticipation can accelerate the situation and cause symptoms of depression, and, in some cases, mood swings.

My Professor of Oncology advised me that, as I had been tested as HER2 positive, the new breakthrough drug called Herceptin, which had not yet been approved by NICE (the National Institute for Clinical Excellence) - the body responsible for approving all new drugs - could be an option. It was suggested by NICE that Herceptin had not been fully tested and was too expensive for national distribution on the NHS. Yet somehow, my wonderful Professor got me on the trial as the first patient in the UK. I was prescribed a course of three weeks on treatment, then one week off by intravenous drip for a twelve-month period. After completing this year long course, I was duly scanned again and the results showed I was clear. How amazing. I was a survivor again as it was not my time to go yet.

Following this wonderful news, Roche, the chemical company who developed Herceptin, asked me if I would be interested in relating my experience of the treatment at a conference for professors and oncologists in Brussels.

I was stunned to be asked but felt that if my case could demonstrate to medical experts that Herceptin had given me another chance of survival and worked, it had to be worthwhile for them to prescribe it to others to aid their recovery. It may also hasten NICE to approve it for those who could not afford it.

So off I went. I arrived at the hotel and was ushered through to the conference hall, where I saw rows and rows of chairs set out in a theatre style layout. It quickly became packed.

I had not really taken on board the daunting prospect of standing in front of hundreds of educated medical experts, oncologists, scientists and professors to speak ad-lib to them all about my perspective as the patient.

I talked about how it had affected me, my family and, more importantly, what hopes this breakthrough drug had given me and what it could do for others. I spoke about why it should become available on the NHS.

I was taken aback by the emotional reception I received as so many medical experts came to me afterwards with tears in their eyes, saying how much they had been moved by my speech. They had never met a patient with the willpower and determination to beat the most aggressive cancer, as I had, and survive it. It is as much taking the drugs prescribed as, at the same time, having the determination, fight and positivity to beat it. I was just determined to be there for my family, come what may.

Once home, we were contacted by London Tonight and Sky TV to do an interview to help spread the word. I was interviewed and appeared on National TV. The camera crews came to our house to film me, which felt oddly quite natural. I was promoting the cause to make this drug available to thousands of people on the NHS, who were not able to get it without paying but who could not afford to do so.

This was such a worthwhile cause for me to be involved in, and if it just helped one other person survive, it would be worth it. Of course, it ultimately helped thousands as, after a year, Herceptin was approved by NICE and distributed by the NHS to all HER2 positive patients, helping so many to survive.

Finally, before attending a charity ball for HEAL (Herts, Essex and London) cancer charity, of which my Professor was the patron, I was invited to do an interview, and have a full makeover for the ball, which would then be published in Woman's Own Magazine. I felt like royalty to say the least. It was a wonderful experience after enduring such trauma that had almost killed me in the process.

I was introduced to two other patients, one a Scottish lady called Liz in her mid- fifties, who had breast cancer, and to a beautiful young blonde girl called Julie, in her early twenties, who had skin cancer.

Together, we had a makeover, and they took before and after photos for Woman's Own Magazine, along with an article about our individual fight to overcome cancer. We really had a wonderful day, and laughed, giggled and compared our histories with each other. We even arrived at the ball with photographers taking our photos as if we were celebrities. Indeed we were celebrities because we had made it through and were survivors. That evening raised so much money for such a worthwhile cause that I became involved in the Heal Cancer Charity, donating time, personal effects and money wherever I could.

Subsequently, so tragically, after some twelve months, I found out that both Liz and Julie had both had relapses and had not survived. I was devastated, to say the least, as this really brought home to me how lucky I was and how sadly their fight had ended. I managed to catch mine in time by knowing my body, and if any odd aches and pains arose, I would get them checked out instantly. This is what gave me my chance of survival.

I was so upset about the tragic loss of these two lovely ladies. Julie had adored sitting in the sun to get a golden tan, and as a result she developed a mole which was malignant and which ultimately struck off a beautiful young life. So to all those ladies out there who are sun worshippers, don't do it. It makes your skin wrinkled, ages you, and can kill you.

Liz, who had breast cancer, had a secondary, and sadly she left her family behind too. For all these ladies who are remembered by those left behind, their valiant fight will never be forgotten.

I asked Neville: "Am I considered to be in remission?"

"No my dear, you're not."

"Why not?" I asked startled.

"Because you have had cancer twice now and you are considered to be at a high risk of a relapse."

After this, I began to realise how short life really is. I vowed to start living every day as though it were my last. We made no plans as a family as we lived life for now, not tempting fate for what could be around the corner. At the end of the day, no one knows what will happen, so now, we just worry about the big things. Maybe that is the best thing to do. So often we get caught up with trivial things that are in reality just not worth spending time and energy on. Just live your life for today and focus on the important issues. Spend your precious time with people that count and with whom you can be sincere.

My friends and family told me they couldn't believe how brave and positive I'd been throughout and what an inspiration I was. It wasn't bravery. It was an enduring fight for survival so as not to leave my family behind, come what may, and to beat this terrible disease that hits so many families.

Once again, I had defeated this torturous disease, and I vowed to live on and be with those who cared for me and help any that needed advice. It's a bit like buying a new car, and then everywhere you go, you see the same model. When you've had cancer, all you hear about is other people being diagnosed with it. I would speak to them to help overcome their fears and set their expectations of what would happen in terms of surgery, treatment, recommendations, second opinions and so on. Sometimes this can be a daunting task as you are not a counsellor or a doctor, but just providing experience is hopefully a great help.

CHAPTER 5

By January 2002, another three years had passed. Our son, aged six, was growing up to be a handsome, well-mannered young man, who adored golf and preferred to play it rather than be at school. If he wasn't playing golf, he was watching it on TV or playing it on his computer. He was golf mad.

I was still constantly monitored every three months with routine scans, tests and examinations. Then, during a routine follow up appointment one evening at the Roding Hospital, accompanied by Russell, my Oncology Professor Neville had his usual chat about side effects and how I was feeling before examining me.

"The usual," I said, as really, nothing had changed.

"Up on the couch then," he said. I duly removed my upper clothing in front of a nurse, no longer feeling embarrassed as I'd done this so many times before. Neville felt around my neck, my breasts and under my arms in his usual fashion.

This time, he took too long pressing around the breast area.

"Ow, that hurts," I said.

Still he continued, longer than normal, and I felt that sick feeling in the pit of my stomach.

"What have you found?" I said, barely able to get the words out.

"I can feel a lump in your breast," Russell said.

"Should we go back to see our breast surgeon again?"

"No wait here, I want to get a second opinion. There's a breast surgeon here this evening, and I would like to him to see you now," Neville said, leaving the room.

Russell and I were stupefied. How could this possibly be happening again?

Neville came back into the room accompanied by a grey haired, suited surgeon. Steven was introduced to us. He examined me first, then told me to get dressed. Then both Neville and he continued to examine and point at the x-rays whilst we sat there in disbelief.

"Well, we will run some tests on you, but I don't think it's anything to worry about," said the other surgeon, nonchalantly. "My secretary will book it in for you and call to arrange times."

"OK, thank you," we said as we left, still dazed by this revelation.

Was Steven right that there was nothing to worry about, or was he covering it up until he was sure? I knew there was something though, as Neville was not usually wrong. Surely, it could not have come back a third time?

The following day, I went to have a CT scan, blood tests and so on, then waited to hear when I would see the surgeon again. The waiting was a killer as I just needed to know if everything was ok. We were on a private health scheme, but it felt like Steven had no sense of the urgency of the situation.

Over a two-week period of prolonged tests and waiting for results, Steven, the surgeon, said he thought it was nothing but could remove the lump anyway. Prior to this diagnosis, we found out that Steven was not actually a specialist breast surgeon, as we had been led to believe, but a general surgeon.

Russell was not satisfied and very unimpressed. So at the next appointment with Steven, he said: "We want the reports and scans of all the tests you have done so far."

"Why?" asked Steven.

"Because I want a second opinion with Lisa's first breast surgeon."

"Well, he won't tell you anything different," Steven said, indignantly.

"Well, we are going to see him tomorrow morning, so I want them now."

Russell was not a person to take fools lightly, being a very strong and determined character, which he needed to be to run his own business. Steven could see that Russell was not going to change his mind, so while not being pleased by our request, he reluctantly gave us the scans and reports.

The following morning, we went back to see my first breast surgeon, Jerry, who looked through the scans and reports that Steven had given us.

"He told us that it was nothing to worry about" I said, furtively.

"Let's examine you then, up on the couch."

Nothing had really changed in this huge room, and Jerry's very direct, strong manner and tone was what I needed to hear as I felt confident of his meticulous ability. He felt around both my breasts.

"Could it have come back after all this time?" I asked.

"My dear, it can come back after any period of time or never resurrect its ugly head. I can however, feel something in each breast and I believe your surgeon Steven does not know what he is talking about. I want to run a couple more tests and then I'll let you know later today what will happen."

We got up with our brains even more muddled and walked out to pass the time until returning later that day.

"Come in, come in," said Jerry. "Well, as I thought, it is not good news as both your breasts are unstable my dear and in my opinion, we are going to have to do a double mastectomy.

"A mastectomy?" I could hardly utter the words. "Isn't there any other alternative?"

"No, it's the best way, you don't want it to come back again, do you? Sleep on it, but this is the only way I can clear the area. You'll have to see another colleague of mine, Jim, who is the best plastic surgeon for reconstruction. I would advise you to see him first before we continue."

Life just flashed by me at this stage. A double mastectomy? No breasts? From being well endowed with large breasts to have nothing was unthinkable to me. I had to have reconstruction, so, robot-like, I made the appointment to see Jim, a silver haired, well-spoken man with a glint in his eyes.

I had already researched him on the internet and found out that his celebrity client list was quite impressive. He told me that Jerry, the breast surgeon, was a close colleague of his and that they often worked together.

"Jerry will get rid of every bit of breast tissue," he said, "and in twelve months' time, I can start reconstruction."

"Twelve months? No, no, I want it done straight away after Jerry has taken away his part," I said.

"That's not advisable" Jim said, "It's better to let the area settle down and heal, then we can rebuild your breasts without any risk of infection. Also, it will be too lengthy an operation if we were to do reconstruction at the same time, I wouldn't recommend it."

"Well, if you think I'm going to wake up from a DD cup to nothing, think again, I would be suicidal," I said, quite without thinking of how I had just spoken to this very experienced plastic surgeon. "I want to have it done at the same time and that's that."

Jim raised his eyebrows, probably never having faced a patient so determined to have it their own way and, moreover, ignoring sound medical advice.

After a minute or two, he said: "OK, well, it will lengthen the duration of the operation, which is not without risk, but if that is what you insist, I'll do it for you."

And so, I was booked in.

The surgery for removing both breasts and reconstruction was approximately nine to ten hours. Russell waited in the room and really didn't think I would make it through as it was such major surgery and it seemed to take forever. This time, he told his Mum that he thought he was going to lose me.

He wouldn't have told my Mum and Dad as they would have been mortified.

Finally, I was taken from the theatre to the Intensive Care room with drips and drains and tubes galore. I don't remember much about it as I was, for the most part, asleep.

From there I was eventually moved to the High Dependency Unit and finally back to my room. I recall looking down at my bandages, but just above them I saw a birthmark on my right breast, which was still there. I couldn't believe it as I thought they wouldn't resemble my original breasts, yet the birthmark was still there. Both the breast surgeon and the plastic surgeons came in after several hours and confirmed that it had been a success.

Over many weeks and months, the breasts were gradually inflated by injections of saline to slowly but surely allow the skin to stretch as the breasts expanded back to my former size. I was advised to consider having smaller breasts, but I refused as this would not be me. I wanted to be voluptuous. I wasn't allowed to wear underwire bras, but just a sports bra to support my new breasts.

I recall having booked a Christmas breakfast at Harrods, many months earlier, to celebrate the Grotto opening with Father Christmas. It was the week after I had come out of hospital. Whilst being very weak and tender, there was no way I was going to let Marc down or our friends whose daughter was coming too. I was only worried that someone might bump into my breasts and that it would hurt. So Russell and our friends stood either side of me, holding my arms, whilst the others walked in front of me to shield me from anyone knocking me. It was a wonderful enchanting morning, with a full English breakfast being served, and Harrods' bears walking around. Finally, our children were taken to the Grotto, and it was lovely to see their faces light up. I was so tired and exhausted afterwards, but it was worth every minute.

The strangest sensation was getting into water and trying to swim – it was impossible as my breasts just did not feel part of me. Slowly but surely I felt better although the numbness lasted a long time.

At the same time I was starting my chemo, my Mum had been having terrible pains in her hip, which severely impacted her walking. I begged her to get it checked out, but she was frightened and nervous, saying to me: "When you are ok, I will get myself checked out."

I said: "No Mum, you are at high risk as I have had it three times."

Her doctor diagnosed her with asthma and sciatica, so we thought nothing of her symptoms as they explained her sighing deeply and her aches and pains when she walked. However, her condition deteriorated, and on further investigation with a CT scan, they said that her hip had been broken, which was a secondary from her lung.

“Secondary?” I said, hardly taking a breath. ‘My darling Mummy had lung cancer. How could this be?”

As I was her only child, she had put all her energy into me and just wanted my good health. Indeed, from the outset, she said she wished it had been her going through cancer and not me. My beautiful Mum had been a smoker of some forty cigarettes per day, and while putting on her makeup in the morning, working or following a meal, she enjoyed smoking.

Thinking back, in the 1940s, it was thought cool to casually hold a cigarette in your fingers and to almost pose whilst smoking. No one realised how serious an addiction it was and how much of a threat it posed on your life. My Mum was a stunning natural redhead with a high back combed set looking hairstyle. ‘carrot top’ they called her at school. She too was meticulous about her appearance as was her Mum, my nanna, who would not go out without her hair or makeup on, even to get a newspaper. It’s funny how this desire to look one’s best, with makeup and hair all in place, continued through three generations.

Mum met and married my dad, who was thirteen years her senior, even though her parents were against the marriage. But, as they say, love conquers all, and so, in 1962, they were wed. Mummy never drove, so daddy was always her personal chauffeur. They spent every day of their lives together, working very hard, playing and holidaying.

Indeed, it was my Dad who had all the major illnesses and mum who nursed him back to health. She looked after the finances and my dad, working, keeping the household in order and cooking delicious meals.

As my Mum’s name was Hilary, my Dad called her his ‘First Lady’, after Hilary Clinton. She had a typical redhead’s temper, and it was not advisable to be around when she lost it. She was loyal, loving, caring and a beautiful individual both inside and out, who adored her family.

So when she became ill, we, her family, fell apart with disbelief. Her dad, my papa, had also been a smoker and died from lung cancer, a terrible, suffering, ending. Surely this could not be the same situation for my mum? There just had to be a cure, a miracle, more time, anything to help her survive. I would not accept no for an answer.

So, for the first time, the BUPA Roding Hospital had mother and daughter in for chemotherapy at the same time. It just had to work. My Mum had also befriended a healer, a religious Christian lady with a calming persona, surely she could help?

We would grab anyone or anything to make her better. But in just six weeks it was all over because it had been left too late. If only we'd got a second opinion earlier about the asthma/sciatica diagnosis. If only I had not taken no for an answer when seeking to get her checked out, maybe, just maybe, she would still be here.

After she passed away, I would look out of the window, watching the world continue as if nothing had changed. Didn't they realise it had? How could life continue as it had before? How would my dad, who relied on my mum for everything, survive? He was mortified as we all were. She'd been his partner and soulmate and now she had gone in what seemed like a flash. How was this possible?

The funeral was terrible. So unbearable. So final. We just wanted her to be with us always, and not just the memory of an exceptional person. How could we all go on without her?

Friends and family were so supportive, but a huge void, a huge empty hole, remained in our hearts. My dad stayed with us for three weeks; we sat and remembered all the memories we shared. We would laugh and we would cry. Mostly, we cried.

We woke and thought that it was all a dream. Then the harsh reality of the situation hit us. My dad returned home as he wanted his independence back, so I had to teach him how to use everything in the kitchen by putting Post-it-notes on everything as he had never done it before. The only thing he'd prepared in a kitchen previously was doorstep-sized cheese sandwiches and cups of tea, so it was quite a project for him. Thank goodness, dad had his car, and slowly, he learnt how to shop for food and look after himself with my help.

Being an only child, I was inconsolable and was cajoled into seeing a psychologist to help me with my grief. I remember going and just breaking down each time. I would steal a look at my watch, or even hers, so as not to look obvious, and wonder how long it would take before it was over. In reality, I didn't feel any benefit from it until the final session, when she said a single line that hit home to me: "Lisa, you know your Mum lives on through you."

This reality comforted me.

It made me realise that Mum is always with us. She's not missing out on our lives. We're missing out by not seeing her, talking to her or cuddling her, yet she lives on through me. So, in turn, I must live on for my son, my family and friends.

Yet again, we felt Mummy had been misdiagnosed with asthma and sciatica, yet it was her determined wish not to get checked out until I was better. To this day, I wish I had pushed her to get it checked out as just maybe if they'd found it in time, as they had with me, they would have been able to do something. On the other hand, lung cancer is known as 'the silent killer' and the only way to find it out is if you develop breathlessness, a cough or a pain somewhere and then insist on an x-ray, which would show anything untoward.

Once again it occurred to us that I too had been misdiagnosed, and while we considered pursuing Steven, the general surgeon, we decided there was no point wasting both energy and time. We knew we wouldn't get anywhere as we had been there before.

Life was never ever the same, yet somehow we all continued through anniversaries, birthdays, Christmas, parties and so on. My dad, amazingly, became very independent, and looked after himself and his house. I also give him my top-up shopping list to keep him active. Thankfully, he drove and even picked up Marc from school, and by keeping his mind and body active, he retained his youthful looks and a working brain.

Chapter 6

In April 2010, another eight years had elapsed. Marc, our son, was fourteen, a typical teenager and still passionate about golf. He had been a county player for three years. He even represented his country Great Britain, playing golf in America and winning gold medals twice. He lived, breathed and played golf every day, telling us: "golf is my life." When asked by anyone what he wanted to do when he left school, he said: "I'm going to be a professional golfer and play on the circuit." When asked, what was his back-up plan was, he said: "I'm going to be a professional golfer." Just like his father, he was single minded, focused and determined.

We now had another member in our family, a black and white Shih Tzu dog called Bentley, who we got when he was just eight weeks old. Bentley was a pedigree, with enormous eyes, and he was the smallest of the litter. Russell had been brought up with cats and was very anti-dogs as he thought they smelt and were not conducive to our lifestyle - that of travelling. He thought they were too much of a responsibility.

One day, my girlfriend Debra bought her white Westie, called Rosie, over to play in the garden with Marc, who was as desperate to have a dog as I was.

I had been brought up with dogs and knew they made a family. Just before my seventh birthday, mum and dad asked me what I wanted for my birthday. I thought long and hard, and said I either want a baby brother or a sister or a dog.

They rushed straight out to the kennels and bought me a dog called Chutch (because he had a chutchie face). He lived for 13 years.

So when Marc and I asked Russell for a dog, he was very anti for almost two years until my girlfriend brought Rosie, her Westie, over to play. Marc just lit up like a light bulb, chuckling and giggling away whilst he and Rosie chased each other round the garden.

When Russell got home from work that evening, we confronted him and said:

"We have decided what we want for our birthdays and Christmas."

"What?" said Russell, with eyebrows raised.

"We want a dog," we said in unison. "We've researched the breeds and have decided on a Shih-Tzu as they are small, they don't moult and they follow you around. They were apparently bred by Tibetan monks as they used to sit on their feet to keep the monk's feet warm. They have the most amazing temperament too."

Without coming up for air, we continued: "We've been in touch with the Pedigree Club and they've put us in touch with a breeder who has just had a litter. We can go and see them this evening and if you don't feel comfortable, or like any of the puppies, we'll understand."

We knew full well that when Russell would see those baby puppies and hold one in his hand, his heart would melt.

Russell conceded, so off we drove, out into the depths of Essex, that same evening to find a highly recommended breeder called Ann. When we arrived, there were eight tiny little black and white fur balls with huge eyes that were just so cute and adorable.

We couldn't help but coo over them all, and Russell picked the smallest puppy, which I asked if he could hold. Bentley as we named him, after Russell's favourite car, was so tiny that he fitted - with room to spare - in the palm of Russell's hand. His heart melted instantaneously. Three weeks later, we picked up our new baby, and he instantly became one of us. He was a very spoilt and pampered pooch. Bentley understood everything and was adorable. Through the highs and mostly the lows, he proved to be a wonderful distraction.

I couldn't believe where the time had gone since we had lost Mummy. Not a day passed when I did not think of her, speak or kiss her picture and just wish I could see her again to talk to her, cuddle her and be together again. The expression 'Life goes on' is cruel, yet so true.

I was still being checked every three months by my Professor of Oncology. My mother-in-law Coralie always accompanied me to see him and would crack jokes.

During a routine appointment, he said: "I think we can consider stopping your medication."

"What? But that's my crutch," I said. "Can you guarantee it won't come back even after all this time?"

"That's impossible, my dear. Of course I can't promise that. But you have been on these drugs for over eight years."

"Will it harm me to stay on them?" I asked.

"How old are you now?"

"forty-six." I replied, my heart pounding.

"Mmm, very well, you can carry on without any problem then."

I breathed an enormous sigh of relief. This was short lived though as while examining my left breast, he paused.

"What have you found?" I asked, with my heart in my mouth.

"I can feel something in your breast."

"What is it?" I cried. He carried on pressing deep into my breast. It was quite painful. Also under my arm and into the side of my breast.

"I can feel something Lisa."

No, it could not be possible. I had been clear for over eight years, surely not. I start to tremble and tears fell down my cheeks. I couldn't possibly be back there again. I was incoherent.

Coralie said: "What should we do?"

"We'll do a PET/CT scan first and see what that shows."

As I got to the hospital front doors, I rang Russell from my mobile.

"I think it's come back."

"What? You're not serious, aren't you?"

"Yes." I was sobbing by this time. Coralie drove me home while I cried all the way.

"You don't know for sure, Lisa, it could be just a gland or something. You've been clear for so long, it could be benign."

I knew though. That knot in the pit of my stomach had returned, and that cold fear, after all that time, was back.

I went to the scanning unit two days later with Russell, I had the scan and then returned to Neville for the results two days later. Those two days seemed like two years.

"Well my dear, I'm afraid it's not good news. The scan shows you have an abnormality, which is inside a muscle. I suggest we get you to see Jerry as soon as possible."

"I'll him tonight," I said, rising from my chair, not sure how my knees and legs carried me out, but Russell helped me.

On the journey home, I phoned Jerry's surgery, only to hear a recorded message. It said that they opened at seven in the morning. How would I make it through the night until then?

Thursday September 28 2000

The Mirror 32p

www.mirror.co.uk

Joely nose it is love

FULL STORY: SEE PAGE 3

I pray that I'll see my son grow up

FIGHTING TOGETHER: Husband Russell and son Marc give Lisa the strength to battle her cancer
Picture: ARNOLD SLATER

THREE months after giving birth to her first child, Lisa Brenner was diagnosed with breast cancer.

Although surgery, chemotherapy, and radiotherapy were initially successful, the cancer returned two years later and spread to her lungs.

Lisa had major surgery to remove the tumour and part of her lung, followed by chemotherapy. Now she is pinning her hopes on a new drug which slows the growth and spread of the disease. "I'm hoping it's going to give me a longer chance of survival so that I can see my son grow up," says Lisa, 35, from Chigwell, Essex. "There are no guarantees but it's worth trying and it's giving me a much better quality of life."

Lisa, a businesswoman, had been married for three years and had just given birth to Marc when she discovered a lump in her right breast in April 1996.

Her doctor thought that it was probably a blocked milk duct, but the lump didn't go away. A biopsy detected abnormal cells. When it was removed, it was found to be one of the most aggressive types of breast cancer and it was growing rapidly because of hormone changes during pregnancy and childbirth.

"The surgeon told me that if I'd left it for another month it would have been too late to treat me," says Lisa.

"My world fell apart. Just a few weeks before I had been enjoying life with a wonderful husband and a lovely son. Here I was, 31 years old, being told I had been close to death. It was unreal."

Lisa had a second operation, a segmental mastectomy, to remove breast tissue surrounding the tumour. But because hers was such a virulent form of the disease she needed a six-month course of chemotherapy and 30 daily sessions of radiotherapy.

Eventually Lisa was given the all-clear, and for the next two years she remained in remission. But in December 1998 she developed sharp pain under her right breast. Tests showed a shadow on her right lung — the cancer had returned, more aggressive than before.

The tumour and the upper lobe of her lung were removed, and Lisa spent two weeks in hospital and a month at home recovering. "The recovery period was horrendous. It was difficult to breathe. I was so weak I couldn't do anything."

Onc… again, Lisa neede… chemotherapy, this time much stronger and much more debilitating.

It caused severe side effects, including muscle spasms, nausea, vomiting, headaches, rashes, cramps, weight gain, depression and hair loss. "If I hadn't had my family I'd have given up and committed suicide," says Lisa. "But I know I had to survive to see my son grow up."

After chemotherapy, Lisa was offered Herceptin, a drug which was still being put through trials. Now licensed, it has been hailed as a major breakthrough in the treatment of women who, like Lisa, have the HER2 genetic defect.

Herceptin blocks the HER2 protein, which is found on the surface of some breast cancer cells and stimulates uncontrolled cell growth. HER2 also makes cells more resistant to chemotherapy. "The once-weekly treatment knocks me out for the rest of the day so I just go to bed," says Lisa. "But the rest of the time I feel fine.

"There have been some awful times, emotionally and physically, but I'm a survivor. I've been given a chance, one that I'm determined to grab with both hands."

HEAL and the Helen Rollason Cancer Care Centre Appeal – founded by Helen and Lisa's consultant Dr Neville Davidson – raise money to improve the treatment and support of all cancer patients.

They are hoping to build a drop-in centre where patients can receive counselling as well as a range of therapies to improve their quality of life while fighting the disease.

Donations to HEAL Charity/Helen Rollason Appeal, Room 40, The Cancer Centre, North Middlesex Hospital, Sterling Way, Edmonton, London N18 1QX.

beaten car

And London cancer charity) to transform these three brave women into glamorous 'girls ab

London. Here the plucky trio tell their heartwarming stories...and pass verdict on their se

Lisa Brenner, 35, lives in Chigwell, Essex, with her husband Russell, 35, a company director. They have a four-year-old son, Marc. Shortly after giving birth, Lisa was diagnosed with breast cancer.

I even thought about killing myself

Liz Couper, 44, an admin assistant lives in Newham, east London, with husband Hugh, 43, a labourer. They have tw and Jordan, has two grow from a previ years ago sh with breast

Woman's Own

HARRODS

DISNEY'S
GRAND FLORIDIAN
RESORT & SPA

CORONATION FESTIVAL

ROYAL
WARRANT
HOLDERS
ASSOCIATION

L.C.B

LOUIS VUITTON

TORY BURCH
TORY BURCH

We finally got home, and somehow I had to be calm, especially in front of Marc, our son, until I was sure.

"How did you get on Mum?"

"They are going to run some further tests on me as they want to be sure everything is ok," I said.

"You will tell me the truth Mum, won't you?" he asked, seeing through me.

"Of course I will Marc."

His eyes were so piercing, and I knew he was waiting for more, that he too deep down knew something was wrong.

I relented. "They think they felt something when examining me and so they are going to run some more tests, and I will hopefully know the results in the next day or so," I said, trying to hold it all together.

"OK Mum, don't worry, you will be ok. I am fifteen now, and I want to know everything. Just don't hide anything Mum."

Marc was no longer a little boy but a young man who was very intuitive and level headed. Still, I did not want to tell him everything until I was a hundred percent sure. I didn't want him to worry. That night, after he had gone to bed, I broke down and Russell said: "Look darling, there is nothing we can do tonight, phone in the morning, and we'll see Jerry tomorrow. Until then, don't make your mind up."

"I know you are right but I also know what it is. I've had it so many times before. Why has it come back after all this time? It's been eight years clear and now I'm sure it's back".

"But you don't know that for sure until they do the tests, do you?" he soothed.

That night I could not sleep. I went through every eventuality. How could this be happening again? I was back to all the whys and hows. I could not make any sense of it returning.

Chapter 7

The following morning, blurry eyed, I telephoned repeatedly until they answered, and I was told that Jerry had retired. How could that be? They told me that I could see his right hand man Simon, but he wasn't in until Monday afternoon.

So I had to wait all weekend before travelling up to Harley Street late in the afternoon the following Monday. Walking back into the same regal waiting room, with the glossy magazines and newspapers on a table in the centre, the same pictures, as if time had stood still. Was it a nightmare?

My name was called, and Russell and I walked into the same office Jerry had occupied. A slightly balding, tall surgeon called Simon was already standing with his arm outstretched to shake our hands and greet us.

"Please call me Simon," he said, with a reassuring, pleasant manner. He asked me to recall my history to bring him up to date. He was very charming and sympathetic as I recalled a potted history of my medical surgery and told him that I just wanted it out.

"OK, up on the couch and let's have a look at you then."

That was a familiar line, but by now I had lost all my inhibitions and undressed so he could examine me.

"Mmm, I can't easily find it, I think it must be deep inside and I don't want to press too hard to hurt you. What I propose is that we do an ultrasound to see the exact position, and I would like you to see the top radiographer, who is here next Monday."

"Next Monday? Can't I have it done today?"

"Unfortunately, he's only here on Monday mornings and has already left."

"Can't I have it done any earlier?"

"Yes you can, but I particularly want you to see this radiographer as he is the best."

So once again, I had to wait a whole week to have an ultrasound. It was sheer hell as our minds travelled at a thousand miles an hour. Finally, Monday morning arrived. We were directed downstairs to the scanning unit and Dr Chin, a tall Chinese man, walked in. Simon the consultant joined him. Dr Chin put gel on my breast and went straight to the area.

"OK, I have it, yes, it is very deep inside and hidden within a muscle. If you had not had the PET scan, it would have gone undetected and you would not be here."

"Why has it come back when I have no breast tissue left?" I asked.

"It's a lymph node which has travelled deep inside your breast."

"Well, where do the lymph nodes go?" I asked.

"From you breast up to your neck."

"Well, while you're there, can you look at my neck? I said, tongue in cheek.

What he said next just blew me away. "Oh yes, I'm not surprised, there's one there too".

"Get them out. I want them both out" I screamed.

"We can't," said Simon.

"Why not?" I uttered.

"The one on your neck is on the main artery, and if we tried to remove it, it would either give you brain damage or kill you. It's too dangerous and not an option. Get dressed and come back upstairs to my office."

I was hysterical by now, tears rolling down my cheeks. Russell was trying to digest this information and get me dressed at the same time. How on earth could we possibly be in the same boat all over again? But we were.

We walked upstairs and waited for a few minutes for Simon to be free. He told me that due to the location of the neck one being on my artery, and the breast one deep inside, there would be no point operating on the breast one and leaving the neck one there.

At this stage, he wanted to speak to Neville, my Oncology Professor, and talk it over with him. He asked us to wait in the waiting room. By now, we were like zombies, staring into space, waiting to find out what would happen.

A few minutes went by and the nurse came over to tell me that Simon had been unable to contact Neville, that perhaps he was in clinic and could we come back later?

"Come back later", I said. "You must be joking. I'm not moving. I'll wait here until he gets hold of Neville."

The nurse looked quite taken aback by my immovable determination.

"Ok. I'll call you as soon as we make contact."

After about five minutes, our names were called again, and we returned to Simon's office.

"I have just spoken to Neville and we've decided the best course of action is to start you on chemotherapy again. He will see you tonight at 6pm to discuss this with you. Please keep in touch and if you have any questions, please call me anytime."

"Thank you," we said, somewhat glumly.

It was mid-afternoon, and as we left to drive home, my mobile rang. It was Neville's secretary Lisa, who told me Neville was going to have a chat with me at our local Bupa Hospital in Buckhurst Hill, and was going to start chemotherapy at 9am the next morning.

"That soon?" I gasped.

"Yes, we know you well Lisa and that you don't like to hang around."

"Yes, but is it that serious to start straight away?"

"Yes," she whispered.

Everything was suddenly happening so quickly, it was hard to absorb it all and it was very frightening. There was going to be no delay because it was life threatening. How much more of this could we endure? All I could think of was Marc.

"How are we going to tell Marc now?" I asked Russell.

"Don't worry, I'll tell him," he said. "I don't want you falling apart."

"I think we should both tell him," I said.

We raced back, getting caught in rush hour traffic, as usual, and made it home with an hour to spare before my appointment. Marc was busy doing his homework and perked up as we walked in.

"Well, how did you get on with the ultrasound? Was it all clear?" he asked.

"Give us a minute to get settled, and then we'll tell you all about it over a cup of tea in the lounge, Marc," said Russell.

I was dreading it.

"Marc, you know mum has been going through lots of tests. We've finally got the results and she has to have more chemotherapy from tomorrow as the cancer has come back."

I'll never forget Marc's face as his jaw dropped with his mouth open and his eyes opened wide.

"How long have you known?" he asked.

"Marc, we really only found out for sure today, but just as I have got over it in the past, I am going to do it again this time."

"Why are they doing the chemo so quickly?"

Very astute.

"Because you know how I like things to be done straight away so that I can get back to normal," I said, quick as a flash.

In reality, I hadn't wanted Marc to worry until we knew for sure what it was and whether they would operate or give me treatment.

"I am fifteen, you know Mum, I can take it," he said.

"I know darling, but we just had to be sure what it was and what they planned before we told you for sure."

"Mum, I'm here for you, I will support and help you all the way," he said, taking my hand.

I do not know, to this day, how I held back the tears. My baby was now a handsome young man, who I loved and adored, and who was now looking after me. It's funny how you bring up your children, tend to their every whim and when you get older, roles reverse. Instead of crying, we hugged each other for a long while.

We saw Neville later that evening and he confirmed that it was serious and that's why they were proceeding so quickly.

"Are you sure you can get rid of it?"

"My dear, I would not be giving you the chemotherapy if would not help you. You'll be ok. We'll give you a six month course of the strongest chemotherapy we can administer along with a new breakthrough drug called Avastin, which will work very well with the type of tumours you have."

"Will there be many side effects?"

"No, not really, just numbness in the fingers and maybe in the feet."

I later discovered this was a major understatement, and I should have focused on the words 'the strongest chemo'.

"What about my hair?"

"It will come out."

"What all of it? What about an Ice Pack?"

"No I don't like to use them as they're more trouble than they are worth. They can cause soreness of the scalp and be very painful."

"OK," I said, and before leaving, I went to have a blood test.

CHAPTER 8

The following morning, we returned to the hospital. It felt like I was going back in time. All the nurses and staff recognised me and were so friendly. All I wanted was to be out of there as soon as possible. As a day case patient, I had a cannula fitted, which is not pleasant, and then a drip with various bags of saline to flush through, plus a whole cocktail of drugs - steroids, chemo and more - to stop me feeling sick and to slow me down so that my blood pressure did not go off the scale. The fluid intake took about three and a half hours, with me falling asleep in the middle due to the strong Piriton dose.

By the time it was all over and I had been unplugged, I was helped by Russell, who had been on his computer the whole time of course, back to the car and home. Russell also carried the carrier bag of drugs for anti-sickness, mouth ulcers, pain killers, morphine and much more.

By the time I was home, I just wanted to sleep. What I didn't realise was what would follow in terms of side effects - not just numbness in the hands and feet as suggested.

In fact, the side effects were so traumatic that I marched back into my oncologist and said: "You lied to me."

His eyes opened wide, yet he still had a slight grin.

"What about?" he said, with a glint in his eye.

"You told me I would just have numbness in my fingers and toes, but it's so severe. It feels like someone has taken an axe and cut off all my toes and chopped up my feet, and the same with my hands and fingers.

"I have had spasms in my back so acute that I've been pinned up against the wall, and my entire body has gone into spasm."

"Nerve endings my dear. I'll give you medication to help calm it down. It's all perfectly normal."

Whilst calming down and realising it was normal to have these nerve ending problems, I thought in the back of my mind: how am I going to put up with six months of this torture? And indeed, I experienced torture like I never had before.

So bad were the spasms in my back that I was forced to give up driving for a year. I hated depending on family and friends to pick me up and take me out. So severe were the pains that I did not have a head to cook. So my amazing friends prepared wonderful meals for us as a family. They were all so unbelievable, and I thank them for all they did to support me.

I finally got into a pattern where my energy was ok in the mornings, and then from 3pm onwards, I would plummet and need to take an afternoon sleep for three to four hours. I felt like an old lady, really, by having afternoon naps. It was good to get into a routine, knowing I would be able to watch some TV, then sleep and wake just before dinner time. This ultimately affected our social life as the only time we could see friends was during the day. I was too tired and zapped of my energy in the late afternoon and evening.

Once again, some three to four weeks into my chemo treatment, my hair started to fall out whilst running my fingers through it or touching it. When more fell onto my pillow, I was mortified and distressed all over again. I called my lovely friend Steven, who was a hairdresser. He decided to cut it very short almost like Mia Farrow, except I did not have her face or figure. So when I lost more hair, it was not as noticeable because it was already short.

I decided to invest in a couple of new wigs, still disbelieving I was back in this position again. But when I wore the wig for the first time, a young sales lady was staring at my hair, and I thought, oh no, here we go.

She said: "Excuse me, I hope you don't mind me asking, but is your hair tinted or highlighted?"

Quick as a flash, I said: "highlighted."

When I came out of the shop, I told Russell and giggling, said: "She would have had a shock if I had taken my wig off and looked at the label to see what it was."

We laughed so much I soon forgot about all my inhibitions. Indeed, my friends said my wigs were better than my own hair. The only benefit was how much quicker it was to get ready by putting a wig on and just running your fingers through it, whereas before I had to blow dry my hair every day. This time, not only did my hair fall out but also my eyelashes and eyebrows, plus what little body hair I had in general. So everything ended up being painted, drawn on or stuck on as before. It took time to look like the old me but was well worth it as everyone treated me normally and said how amazing I looked.

I really don't know how I managed to get through this torturous chemo, with so many awful toxic side effects, but, somehow, each day was one day closer to finishing the course of treatment. My body felt like it had been pummelled by a boxer, and my energy levels were so low. Yet I was still so determined to win and be there for our son, my husband, family and friends. I was not going to give in, and while I knew I was ok in the mornings, I forced myself to go out and do as much as possible before giving into my rest time.

Six months passed, and in October 2010, I finished my chemo. I went to see Professor Neville to find out if I would need radiotherapy. He told me he would like me to see a colleague of his called Nick, who was the leading authority on Cyberknife surgery.

"What's that?" I asked.

"It's a leading-edge brand new technology delivered by a robot, very focused radiotherapy, accurate within millimetres."

So an appointment was set up for me, and I went back to Harley Street with Russell to meet Nick. While reading through the referral letter from Neville, he asked me a number of questions, and I asked lots back in return – I was very good at making lists of questions as this stage. He explained that it was not automatic that I would qualify for Cyberknife as only patients with inoperable tumours were automatic candidates. He told me to call his secretary in a week's time. I was taken aback as I had assumed this was automatic, but instead my history and details were to be put before his medical team for approval.

There was also some controversy whether the tumour in my neck, preventing me having surgery, was still there or not. So during that week, when I was waiting for the verdict of approval, I was also waiting to see if the neck tumour had gone or not. Very stressful to say the least.

Finally, the following week came round, and the first thing that Nick advised was that the neck tumour on the scan was no longer active and was scar tissue.

"Are you absolutely sure?" I asked.

"See the radiographer's report for yourself," he said, turning the printed piece of paper round for me to read. "The good news is that you do qualify as a candidate for Cyberknife, so have a chat with Lisa, one of my team, and she will book it in for you."

Just as simple as that. Yet in the back of my mind, I thought that if the inoperable tumour in my neck had definitely gone, then perhaps I should have the one in my breast surgically removed.

The following morning, I spoke to Lisa and ran through all the details regarding this breakthrough technology that I had forgotten to ask Nick. She was very nice and duly answered everything. The only thing that stayed in my mind was that she said:

"Don't be dismayed, but some of our patients have been distressed to see the tumour is still there following the treatment."

This was the rod that broke the camel's back. I wanted the treatment as it was not invasive, but if the tumour was to stay inside me, I didn't want it to remain in my body.

"But why does it stay there?" I asked.

"You will need to ask Nick that."

Both Russell and I felt that we were back to square one again. How could we have this treatment if the tumour was left inside your body? After prolonged thought, I decided to ring Simon, the breast surgeon, and go see him, with a view to removing the tumour in my breast. He was off sick, so I rang every day to be told he would be back the following week.

When I finally arranged the appointment, we were shocked to see he had a cast on his arm.

"How did you do that?" we said, stunned.

"I was feeding a horse and then another one came at the side of me and got the needle and kicked my arm. It was so painful, but the cast should be off in a couple of weeks' time."

Another couple of weeks. Was anything able to be done right now?

I explained that I had been approved to have Cyberknife surgery but that the tumour would remain in my body. I wanted surgery to get it out, and as the neck one was just scar tissue, that to me, it was just better to get it over with.

"Hmm," said Simon. "Let's get another ultrasound done to see the position of the chest tumour. Dr Chin is in today, so come downstairs with me now and let's have a look."

Both Simon and the radiographer took time to locate the site, and when they finally did, they both studied the location. I returned to Simon's office.

"Well, it's very deep and not easy to reach. Also, I'm not sure that surgery is ideal."

"Why?" we asked.

Simon paused and appeared not to want to say what he next said. What he did say blew us away. "I'm not really happy and want to get a second opinion."

Once again, we asked why.

"To get to it, I think we would have to remove all the organs blocking it, sever them from the main arteries, then remove the tumour and reconnect all your organs."

Russell and I sat there, with mouths open, aghast to think of what the ramifications could be.

"Even if I could get to it to remove it for you, I can't do it because of the break in my arm, but I know a woman who can, and maybe she can bypass removing all the organs."

"Who? Is she any good?" I said.

"Well, if my wife needed surgery, she'd be the only person I would go to."

That was good recommendation in itself, so I agreed to return the following Monday to see Fiona.

"Lisa, I don't think you can have the surgery, I think you should have the Cyberknife as it's non-invasive," Russell said. "If you have surgery and they do what Simon said, there is a risk of your arm not working at all as all the organs have got to be reattached, and what happens if something goes wrong? You could be disabled darling, and that's all we need."

"Yes, but with Cyberknife the tumour stays in the body, and I want it out. Think we should wait and see what Fiona says on Monday?"

I think I changed my mind about surgery and Cyberknife a hundred times, but we were both dependent on making a decision once we had met Fiona. That weekend was mind destroying as I felt like I had opened up a can of worms by looking at all the possible options.

The following Monday, we walked into a smaller office to meet a very well-manicured lady surgeon.

"Oh, so you're the complicated lady then, are you?" were the first words she said to me.

"Yes it seems I am."

"Well, let's have you up on the couch then and see what it looks like."

Fiona was very adept at what she did as she used an ultrasound and went directly to the location.

"OK, I have it. Alright, you can get dressed now," she said.

I duly did so and returned to sit next to Russell. "What do you think?"

"I must tell you that I do not want all Lisa's organs detached and reattached as it is too much of a risk," said Russell.

"Well, I had a lady much like Lisa just over a month ago, and she also had an inoperable tumour, which entailed removing organs. She didn't want that, the same as yourselves. However, when I opened her up, I managed to get to it without removing anything. I think I could try and do the same for you, but until we open you up and have a look, I can't promise anything."

"What if you can't?" I said.

"Well, then I would have to sew you back up again."

Russell and I looked at each other. What should we do?

Seeing the worried, anxious expressions on our faces, she said: "Look, you don't have to make a decision now, talk it over and think about it over the weekend. You can always phone me back next week."

Part of me wanted to say ok there and then as she seemed so confident and skilful, and we had to make a decision as all we were doing was going backwards and forwards. Yet what if she could not reach the tumour?

CHAPTER 9

All weekend we discussed the pros and cons, and decided we should speak to the Cyberknife team again before making a decision. The decision was whether to have invasive surgery that may or may not be successful, or non-invasive Cyberknife that could leave the tumour inside my body.

Typically, we were unable to contact Nick, the Cyberknife man, but finally we spoke to him, and he confirmed that though the tumour would still be present in my body, the activity would be gone, and the tumour would biodegrade, in time, in the body.

On hearing this, we both decided that Cyberknife was the way to go, and if for any reason it didn't work, we had the option of surgery to fall back on.

As Russell said: "Lisa, if you had the surgery, went through all the trauma and general anaesthetic, and then woke up after to be told it hadn't worked, how would you feel?"

"I would be mortified," I said.

"So there you have it," said Russell. "We have to go for the non-invasive route, and at least we will have the back up of surgery if Cyberknife doesn't work."

While we had gone all round the houses searching for the right way forward, we had at last come to a decision. Now in my normal fashion, I wanted everything done now.

I received a call from the Cyberknife team who booked me in and answered my many questions. I was advised I would only need three treatments, but there was some preparation before. So I went with Russell and Marc one cold winter morning, with snow covering all the pavements and roads.

It had been raining the night before, so all the pavements were treacherous. Holding onto each other in case one of us should slip, we arrived at the Cyberknife clinic in Harley Street. We were taken to the basement, to a room where we were advised that a mould would be made of my upper torso so that I would be unable to move on the table and that, as the robot was accurate within millimetres, this would be the most comfortable way for me to lie on the bed for two or three hours each time.

"Can we see the robot?" asked Russell.

"Yes, of course you can, it's just next door."

We got up and followed the administrator. We were shown to a very clinical, white theatre style room, with a huge floor to ceiling robot that rotated it's long winch arm so that it could give rays above and below the bed which I would lay on.

I have to say, it was awesome, to the point of Marc saying "wow."

The Cyberknife lady asked Marc to wait for us outside this room as no doubt she must have thought it would be too daunting for him, plus I guess there were health and safety issues too. We were dumbfounded by all this technology.

We had found out that Cyberknife surgery, which is currently the latest technology, costs two or three million pounds per robot. They are designed to give the most accurate radiotherapy - within millimetres - for inoperable tumours, predominantly in the brain or the spine.

As mine was deep inside the chest wall, hidden inside a muscle, the Cyber team met to agree if I was a suitable candidate, so it was not quite given that I was going to be automatically accepted. When I was accepted, I was ecstatic. To make the mould, I lay on an impregnated cloth that they pulled around my shoulders and waist, which then set in place. This was what I lay in on the bed to make it more comfortable and so that I couldn't move so the rays would penetrate the exact location. It was a very intimidating experience as this huge robot almost appeared to come up to my nose to angle itself at my chest. This process took two or three hours, with multiple positioning of the robot around my body. I just had to shut my eyes and listen to my IPod, otherwise I would have hyperventilated and been out of there.

The only invasive part of this treatment was the preparation of inserting three or four gold markers, placing them onto the tumour inside the breast under local anaesthetic by going in and out of a CT machine repeatedly. This was not at all pleasant as huge needles were protruding from my breasts.

Russell asked: "Can we have the gold after you've finished doing the Cyberknife?"

Ever the businessman, as scrap gold was at an all-time high.

"No unfortunately not, as the markers stay in the body permanently," replied the nurse.

"Won't I bleep if I go through the scanner at the airport?" I asked.

"No, it's gold, so it won't affect it."

After three day's treatment, ending on New Year's Eve, I had to wait three months to have a repeat PET scan to find out if it had worked.

I had been recommended to two angelic healers called Su and Francis, an adorable couple, so genuine, so gifted and so understanding, who were put in touch with me by my girlfriend Debra. They came to my house every Wednesday evening, and we became friends.

After I had finished my Cyberknife treatment, they told me that they could not feel anything bad. When I finally had my PET scan, some three months later, I returned to my oncologist, Neville, for the results. I was nervous and anxious to find out if the combination of oral chemotherapy and Cyberknife surgery had worked. In his usual fashion, Neville turned the report round for me to read myself. I scanned through all the technical jargon to see a line that read: 'I am pleased to report that there is no longer any activity and that the patient is in remission'. Remission? I had never been told at any time during fifteen years that I was in remission. Wow.

"Unbelievable," was all that I could utter. Then I threw myself into Neville's arms, and kissed him and thanked him for saving my life once again.

"You are a walking miracle," he said. "It is so nice to have a happy ending. Most patients such as yourself do not make it through the second time and you have fought it bravely four times. The ones that come into my office crying do not survive. Your determination and positive attitude to be with your family has made you a survivor."

"Yes, but not without the brilliant team Lisa has around her, including you Neville," said Russell.

"Please, can I have a copy of the report?" I asked.

"Yes, of course my dear, you can take this one, I have already had it copied for you."

"Thank you Neville, for saving my life again, you are never allowed to retire," I said.

"Is there any more treatment Lisa will need?" asked Russell.

"Yes, I'm going to put her on oral chemotherapy tablets. They won't have the same severity of side effects as the intravenous chemo and can be administered at home: two weeks taking the tablets, one week off."

"How long will I need to take them for?"

"About five years," said Neville.

This news did not seem to matter as all that was important was that the treatment had worked.

We walked out of the hospital on cloud nine. Indeed, I felt like skipping. Had he really said that? I looked down at the report he had given me and read it over and over, tears rolling down my face. The first phone call I made was to Marc. Whilst waiting for the phone to ring and connect, I composed myself.

"Marc, it's me."

"Well, did you get the results, Mum?"

"There is no more activity darling, the chemo and Cyberknife have worked."

"That's fantastic news, Mum," Marc said, with a huge lump in his throat.

We both cried with joy.

"I still have to be on medication and take chemo tablets, but none of that matters as the cancer has gone."

"Oh Mum, I'm so happy, that's the best news ever."

Indeed it was. I called my dad and Coralie and then texted my wonderful news to all our friends. My mobile was red hot with exclamations of joy at this fantastic news. I knew I was not out of the woods but having this result was amazing.

I would have to be on chemo tablets for five years which sounded a really long time, but if you consider, as one of my friends told me, that's five years of keeping the cancer away.

CHAPTER 10

We had totally underestimated Marc, who we thought was an average student until such time as he did his GCSEs. He sat twelve subjects and passed all with excellent grades. Following this, he decided to continue at college taking a Triple Sports BTech which was the equivalent of three A Levels. Not only did he finish the course a year early but achieved triple distinction star, the equivalent of three A stars. Incredible.

As a result of this and his continued love of golf, Marc turned professional at the age of just seventeen and was offered a place at Birmingham University a year early to take a degree in the PGA (Professional Golfers Association). We were and are so proud of him.

In December 2013, I went for my normal three months check up with my Professor.

"Well, I think you're due for your annual PET scan my dear, come back and see me afterwards, and I'll give you the results."

There was no urgency in his voice, so I booked the scan for the following week and left a message on the answer phone for Neville's secretary Lisa the following morning to ask the Professor the results.

I duly went about my day on Friday, 13 December and was in Morrison's with Coralie doing my regular shop. My phone rang, and it was Lisa.

"Hi Lisa, is everything ok?" I asked.

"The Professor would like to see you now at Springfield Hospital, how soon can you get there?" My heart sank.

"What, now?" I exclaimed.

"Yes," she said, quietly.

I did not even need to ask her, but I still did. Quite professionally, she said she had not seen the report, but I knew deep down that she had.

I told her I would call Russell and ring her back to confirm the time. I screamed for Coralie, who had another shopping trolley and was down the next aisle.

She came running. "What is it? What's the matter?"

"It's back," I said, with tears running down my face.

We returned home, and my dad and Marc were both occupied. I dumped the shopping and told them we had to go out to get a last minute Christmas prezzie. They looked perplexed and clearly were not sure whether to believe me or not as Russell, Coralie and I zoomed back out of the door. I just felt there was no need for them both to be anxious for the few hours until we had had confirmation one way or the other.

"Where do you think it has come back to?" I asked Russell and Coralie on our way to Chelmsford.

"You don't know for sure it has Lisa," said Coralie.

"There's no other reason why he would want to see me straight way, the same day," I cried.

"Maybe it's your bowel, Lisa, as you've had lots of haemorrhoid problems, and your dad had bowel cancer," Russell said.

"Maybe..." I said, still in horror of what he was going to tell me.

We finally arrived at the hospital and signed in. There was one patient ahead of me, a pleasant looking young man in his early thirties. Finally, my name was called and in the three of us went.

"Well my dear, it's not good news, it's come back."

"Where?" I gasped, hardly able to breathe.

"Your lung, the same one as last time."

"How could it come back again?" I squealed.

"Did you see the young man who left just before you?" Neville asked.

"Yes," I answered glumly.

"I saw him a few months ago, and it has now come back everywhere. Sadly, there is nothing I can do for him."

"Terrible," said Russell.

"So what are you going to prescribe for me?" I asked, already knowing the reply.

"Six months' chemo starting next week at Holly House Hospital."

"But I've been on oral chemo tablets, so why did it come back?"

"Because they stopped working," he answered.

"Well give me the strongest you've got, and let's blast it." Words I would later regret.

Glumly, we walked out of the hospital, with a million thoughts and numbness overtaking us all at the same time because I'd been here so many times before, and it was worse because I knew what lay ahead of me. Indeed, we all did.

"Well, at least they're offering you treatment, Lisa," said Coralie.

"Yes, I guess you're right" I answered, quietly.

We made our way home in troubled silence, and then we had to tell Marc and my dad. They were in total disbelief.

"Look, as they're offering me treatment, you don't have to worry, only if and when there is nothing more they can do, that's the time to worry," I said, and it was so true.

Nonetheless, the trauma and physical endurance of the forthcoming treatment made my heart feel like a lead weight. How could I go through all this again, and why had it come back?

I started my chemo the following Monday, which was two weeks on and one week off, but the side effects proved to be so gruesome and unbearable that I ended going back to hospital to see Neville, who switched me onto another chemo drug.

Yet again this had significant side effects but was only just more tolerable. Every joint in my body felt like it was being chopped off, and I was put onto much stronger drugs for severe neuropathic pains. Yet still it would stop me in my tracks.

CHAPTER 11

From this point onwards, Russell has added some of his own memories to Lisa's writing.

It was coming up to Marc's 18th birthday, in January 2014, and he so wanted us to take him to New York. Everyone thought I was nuts to go, but when you have one child, you want to give them the world. To be absolutely truthful, I wanted him to have good memories as I didn't know what the future would hold.

So with grim determination, I ignored everyone's advice and told Russell that I could just as well be ill there as here, and if I were tired, I could rest in the hotel, and the boys could go and play golf. We cleared it with my professor, who prescribed me Valium and oral Morphine. For this I had to get a medical letter to allow me to travel with it. Knowing that I had unswerving determination, Russell booked, and the following week, the three of us flew to JFK airport, New York.

January is not the ideal time of year to go to New York as it was freezing. However, this did not deter us from shopping till we dropped. The boys practiced their golf at the driving range every day as the courses they wanted to play were closed due to snow.

On the first morning, Marc wanted to go to a diner, and we asked the hotel for recommendations and set to the nearest one. I had not taken my pills as they needed to be taken with food and did not anticipate any problems. However, as we crossed the busy road and stepped on the pavement, my ankle felt like it had been chopped off, and I started to collapse. Russell and Marc grabbed an arm each and thankfully caught me before I fell to the ground.

"You see, I told you we shouldn't have come," said Russell.

"I'll be fine, just get me to the diner, and I'll take my pills with breakfast," I retorted.

We got to the diner, and I slumped into the booth and got my pills ready.

"Stop looking at me, I'll be fine. I just need to pace myself and take my pills regularly."

"Mum, I'm sorry, I feel so guilty," Marc said, glumly.

"Don't be. I was wrong not to have taken my pills before we left the hotel. I wanted to come just as much as you, and I want the three of us to make a list now of all the things we want to see and do."

So that's where we started our trip to celebrate Marc's 18th, his coming into adulthood. Our friends from West Palm Beach, who had two sons, flew in to join us, staying at a different hotel just around the block. It was lovely to spend time shopping and eating with them too.

Marc had a fantastic time and literally shopped till he dropped. I bought some sparkly UGG boots and tops in keeping with my bling wardrobe. January in New York is very cold but there were bright sunny skies, and it was beautiful as ever. We ate, walked miles and shopped as though our lives depended on it. Marc practiced his golf at Chelsea Piers driving range every day. Such an amazing trip.

CHAPTER 12

We returned to the UK, and I resumed chemo every three weeks when my Prof recommended I return to Harley Street to see if I was eligible for Cyberknife treatment on my lung. In addition, I was also to have a lung ablation and would need gold markers inserted inside my lung for the robot to focus the treatment on again.

There was a whole process for approval by a panel, who accepted on the basis it would be successful in zapping it.

We had arranged to meet Robert, Marc's godfather, and he met us in Harley Street.

While he was waiting, I was there having the pre scans, and I was asked if I would have a biopsy on my neck done. It seems that during the scan on my lung they had seen something on my neck, and they wanted to check this further.

"Would you like us to do it now?"

"Yes," I said, nonchalantly, not realising what was involved.

I asked Russell to come into the small theatre, and while laying on the table, I leaned over to Russell and said: "stay here and hold my hand."

I think I crushed his fingers as I didn't realise how uncomfortable and painful a neck biopsy would be. It felt like I was being strangled and held down at the same time. Not pleasant at all.

Finally, the results came back, and I was referred to a neck surgeon who confirmed I had a malignant thyroid.

What next? There was quite a procedure to say the least, and not without pain or infection, but finally was successful.

CHAPTER 13

In 2014, I was sitting down one evening, trying to relax, when Russell suddenly yelped. I panicked, raising both my feet off the floor, believing there to a spider or, worse still, a rodent.

"What's the matter? What have you seen? " I asked, panic stricken.

"Nothing, I can't see," said Russell.

"What do you mean? Which eye?"

"I can't see out of my left eye. Don't worry, I have an appointment tomorrow with the optician, so I'll get him to check it out. I need to get my vision checked out again. Actually, I can feel pressure behind my eye."

Why pressure? Russell must need a new prescription.

The next day, Russell went with Marc to the optician whilst I ran out to get the weekend food shop. He reappeared with a letter which reported the scan.

To cut a long story short, Russell had a big green mass behind his left eye. He was referred to an Ocular Oncologist, which is an eye oncologist. Apparently, it is a very rare condition and if malignant, requires invasive treatment surgery, risking loss of sight or loss of his eye. So very risky.

Fortunately, we were referred to the top female ocular oncologist, who happened to be the director of Moorfields Eye Hospital. She conducted various tests for eye cancer.

How could both husband and wife be diagnosed with cancer at the same time? What would we tell Marc? He would be mortified as both parents had cancer.

We decided not to tell him until it had been confirmed, and sure enough, it was verified.

Over the Christmas period of 2014, I started to have the Cyberknife treatment again and had to encounter this knowing that in January I would need thyroid surgery to remove the cancer.

I always felt that I was going to survive and this is what I had to do. I think the hospital was amazed at seeing me all made up, looking sparkly with bling, and getting on with it. I was fine as I had Russell by my side and knew we would get through this.

CHAPTER 14

In January 2015, I went in to have surgery to remove the thyroid cancer at the King Edward VII Hospital. I was advised that I may lose my voice, but we would not know until after the surgery. At the same time, I was advised that I would need radiotherapy later. Whilst all this was going on, I was worried about Russell as he also needed to have eye surgery, but he was concerned with me to make sure I was alright. So there we were, worrying about each other. It seems ridiculous, but all we could think of was our son.

We battled on. Russell was putting off the surgery because of me, but his surgeon advised it had to be done and couldn't wait any longer. At the same time, I was advised that I needed further radiotherapy, and I would need a mask made up for this, so they could work directly on the cancer.

So in July 2015, Russell had surgery, and I was beside myself with worry as was Marc. They were unable to move the tumour for Russell, but he was treated with radioactivity and that really was the best they could do. The following week, I was in for further treatment, so one week it was Russell and then the following week myself. I had to have radioactive iodine treatment to try and clear me from any cancer.

At this time, I had to be left at a different hospital in London, shut into a room with no-one allowed in for 24 hours. The whole experience was necessary as advised by the team, like a clear up I believe.

I was then allowed to get on with my life, and even though I had encountered all the different items during the year, I actually felt everything was looking good. We planned a holiday with our Marc in September and went to the USA. My life was normal again, but this time, I felt that we were going forward. I had had everything thrown at me, and here I was surviving.

A month later, in October, one of our friend's parents passed away, and as I walked to the house, I fell and cut both my legs. I walked into the house, bleeding, but luckily, there was a doctor friend of ours who sorted me out. I thought it was the actual paving, but the following evening and after having had a brain scan beforehand as a routine check-up, I visited my professor. He asked how I had been. I said fine apart from the fall.

It was then on the 8th October 2015 that I was diagnosed with three brain tumours, and I would need daily radiotherapy again with a mask being made up once more. This was the reason I fell, not anything else.

On 24th November 2015, I had an MRI brain scan, and then, on 26th November, I was told that it had gone from three to five tumours, and now there was nothing they could do. My professor was beside himself and just could not believe that after surviving all these years with the intense treatment I had encountered, there was nothing further they could do.

I was given possibly six months to live, but strangely I felt fine. I was due to have chemo the next day and this still happened. I started to use a walking stick, and luckily I had a friend called Lynne who was able to bling it up. This caused a lot of attention, and I loved it.

I was up to eleven times of having had cancer, and now it was in my brain, lung and chest. The next few days, I did not feel good at all, and during the night of the 30th November, I was totally different, not myself. Although I was made up and looked good, I felt completely opposite.

The next day, 1st December 2015, Russell said that I may be better in hospital to be looked after. I agreed and made myself up. For some reason, that day it took me four hours to get ready, and I had to get Russell to help me downstairs.

I managed to pack a hospital bag. When I got downstairs, my dad was there, and he could not understand what was happening. I looked like normal but I wasn't, and Russell told dad that I would be better in hospital and he was going to take me.

On the 1st December 2015, I was taken to the Rivers Hospital, Sawbridgeworth, and on arrival, I could not get out of the car. I seemed to deteriorate on the journey as now I could not move. A porter at the Hospital came and helped me out. He took me in by wheelchair to the room that Russell had organised for me.

Later that day, the professor turned up, and they started to treat me in order to make me more comfortable. I was treated to chemotherapy whilst at the Rivers.

I felt that I was not giving up and that I was going to fight as I had always done. Christmas at the hospital was made up of just three patients including myself, and I was made to feel extremely looked after. I know it was difficult for the family, but they rallied around me.

CHAPTER 15

In January 2016, it was Marc's birthday. He was going to be twenty. I still felt I would be able to fight and actually did not feel ill, even after the chemo. My friends came to visit me. Russell visited me every day, and I had good and bad days.

One day I was actually asleep when Russell came. By the time he left, it was dark from the early winter evenings, and I hadn't actually had dinner. Anyway, I woke up and asked the nurse what time it was, and she said 12:00. I thought it was lunch time, but it was midnight. I had slept right through.

I was now not able to walk due to the cancer, and my brain was not responding correctly with my legs. However, I was given a walking frame and starting to have physio to be able walk again with the use of the frame. My friend Lynne was able to also bling up the frame and that made me want to use it, especially as I was not able to use the blinged up walking stick.

On the day of Marc's birthday, I had my very close friends Amanda and Robert - Marc's godparents - come to the hospital, and when they arrived, I actually lost my balance and fell in my room. Luckily, they did not see this, but all the doctors came to help me, and they had to wait. I did not want Marc to see his mum on the floor.

I was being very well cared for by the Rivers, and the nurses and staff were all amazing with me. It turned out I was their longest serving patient. The time came for me to leave, and on the 14th February, I was able to go home. I felt pleased but maybe a little concerned because I had been used to being in hospital, some twelve weeks in all.

Russell had arranged for a hospital bed and items to be delivered home. When I got home, there were carers on hand to help me, and in fact, my dining room was now my bedroom. I had someone stay with me through the night now, and carers looked after me during the day, as well as Russell. I also had a night carer. This was then increased to two carers, morning, noon and night.

St Clare's Hospice were also visiting on a daily basis, and I don't know how we would have managed without them. But we managed to live as normally as possible.

Russell would take me out, and we managed to go to a wedding the following month. I was not good that day, but still I made up and was absolutely going to go. It was hard, but we got there, and I enjoyed it. Normality is necessary and that is what I wanted to do. I was in a wheelchair, but here I was at the wedding,

I had made it.

CHAPTER 16

A month later, I started to have falls. This happened on two occasions. My dad was helping me on one of them, and I fell. Luckily, Marc was around, and an ambulance was called. They actually needed another ambulance to help get me to A&E.

I was very worried as it was Sunday, and Marc had his final PGA Degree exams the next day. So I was sitting in A&E, and Marc had brought his revision books with him. I could not understand how he managed to revise, let alone take his exams the next day.

The following week I fell again, and the same thing happened but the ambulance crew advised me to stay at home. It was now coming up to the end of April 2016, when my GP suggested that I would be better off going into a local hospice. I was not too happy about this.

In the beginning of May 2016, my GP advised me again that a hospice would be the best place for me as I was not well and they would care for me. I had always said I would not go into a hospice, but Marc, Russell and my GP all thought it was the best place for me. I thought about it, and for the sake of my family and myself, I thought this was, in the end, the best thing to do.

As St Clare Hospice had been visiting me on a daily basis, they agreed to admit me, really for a short period, just to check if they could improve my medication and make me more comfortable.

The Hospice was actually very nice; I had a nice room and nothing was too much trouble for them. The gardens were exceptional and relaxing. I felt OK and never felt like giving up at all. This is how you have to be. I had had cancer eleven times, and yet I still felt fine and wanted to be around for my family and friends.

I actually spent three weeks at St Clare Hospice, then Russell and I discussed our options because you cannot live in a hospice. I agreed to go to the Gardens Neuro Centre on the Rivers Hospital Complex. I knew the area from being in the hospital.

CHAPTER 17

Russell's story

In May 2016, Lisa was given just three weeks to live after arriving at the Gardens Neuro Centre.

Right up to the end, Lisa was still very happy and not upset or depressed at all. She felt that there was no way she was going to give in to cancer or slip away without fighting to the bitter end.

Everyone at the Gardens Neuro Centre were exceptional in keeping Lisa happy and comfortable under the circumstances. I was able to take her out in her wheelchair and into the lovely gardens on site, even to a local pub for lunch and, occasionally, shopping.

Lisa's healer, Francis, visited her every single week, even on Christmas day. Rain or shine, Francis was there, and Lisa loved to see him. As Lisa was glamorous and loved everything bling, she would always want her nails and makeup looking good. With this in mind, I arranged for a nail technician to visit her to make sure she always looked good, so she could in turn feel good. Lisa was at first confined to a wheelchair. Then things changed, and she was eventually bedbound.

It was coming up to Lisa's 51st birthday, and I wanted to do something to make the most of the situation. I did consider a party for her friends to come, but really Lisa was just not up to it.

I organised a room at the home and had this decorated. It was just my mum, Coralie, my brothers Cliff and Warwick, and their kids: Harley, Coco, Oliver and Rocco. And, of course, myself and Marc.

In July, it was Lisa's first cousin's, Lawrence's, funeral. It was difficult for us not to be able to tell Lisa as it would have upset her. It was also hard to go without her. Lisa was very close to her first cousins Sue and Lawrence. Sadly, Lawrence had also passed away from cancer.

In the summer, Marc got the results for his PGA degree, and he passed with top marks. He actually got the results while at the care home. Lisa heard the news from Marc and shed tears of happiness. It was very emotional.

Lisa's cousins, Sue, Mel and Millie, came to visit and a select few friends who Lisa asked to see, like Michaela, her oldest friend, Amanda G and Heather.

Lisa did not want friends to remember her in the state she was in as she was becoming more ill by the day. It was her wish not see to everyone purely because of this.

My mother, Coralie, was very close to Lisa and unfortunately passed away on the 9th November 2016 - on the same day as my father Roland had 35 years before. We didn't tell Lisa at the time because we all felt this would not be good and too upsetting. It was difficult not saying anything at all, but strangely enough, Lisa never asked where my mother was.

Just over a month later, on Christmas Day, I took in presents for

Lisa, but she really was not able to enjoy them. Also, Amanda, Marc's godmother, came to visit, but with Lisa's health being very poor by now, the day was very different to the previous Christmas, and frankly was very difficult for her, and for us to watch.

It was very upsetting seeing Lisa so unwell, but whenever I asked her how she was, she always said fine, and she never complained about anything. The staff often asked me if she was in pain. I asked Lisa, and the answer I always got was no.

She didn't want me to be upset or worried at all. I showed her photos of our life and asked her one day: "what happened?"

The reply I got was: "cancer." It was very upsetting.

Lisa, however, always wanted to see our son grow up and reach twenty-one, and she did.

Marc graduated with his PGA Golf Degree, and it was coming up to his 21st birthday on the 18th January. On that day, I asked her if she could speak to Marc although it was becoming increasingly difficult for her to say anything.

Marc walked into the room, and the first thing Lisa said was: "Happy Birthday."

Marc was astounded, like all of us, and then to top it, Lisa told him: "I love you."

I know this will stay with Marc forever and it was incredible for all of us to see.

So Lisa was able to see Marc on his 21st birthday and also to meet and know his girlfriend Talia over the last eight months.

Even though Lisa was ill, the Gardens Neuro Centre asked her if she wanted the Flu Jab during the winter. She said yes, and the funny thing is, everyone else caught colds, and the only one person that didn't was Lisa - even though Lisa did not have any immunity from all her cancer treatment.

In April 2017, some eleven months from being told she would only survive three weeks, Lisa was unable to eat normally. She could only have soup and yoghurt. In the end, Lisa was not able to eat or drink at all but still tried, and on occasions did manage something, albeit very small. She managed to survive weeks like that.

My brother Cliff wanted to see Lisa. I knew it was likely we would not have long, and when we were in the room, suddenly Lisa actually stopped breathing. We both thought she had gone, but then she started breathing again, fighting hard as ever. Lisa had an inner strength which was truly incredible.

It was coming up to Marc's graduation, so we were all concerned with Lisa now not being well at all. I said that Lisa would have wanted us to attend. We did, and Lisa was greatly missed on this very special occasion and would have been very proud. We did go to the Care home in the evening, but Lisa was too tired and didn't wake up.

I was in her room on Wednesday 3rd May 2017 and popped out to get a glass of water. Nurses were doing a stock check, and I was called into the room. I went in, and I saw Lisa at peace. She had passed away at 3:40pm.

Marc and Talia were already on their way as I had felt Lisa was not in a good way, but when they arrived, it was too late. I feel that Lisa did not want us to see her go, and this is why it happened when no-one was there.

Everybody who met or knew Lisa always developed a fond spot for her as she was genuinely a lovely person, who never had a bad word to say about anyone. I loved Lisa with all my heart. She was the best thing that happened to me.

I believe that Lisa beat cancer surviving 21 ½ years after having had it 11 times from being diagnosed. This book will hopefully give you the same inspiration to beat it if you look at what Lisa did.

CHAPTER 18

Lisa's message after her fourth time of having cancer

So I am now still currently in my first year of taking chemo tablets. The side effects in terms of nerve ending pains are still there, still horrible and accumulative, but you know what? I take my painkillers and put up with the tiredness, more accepting of the fact that there is no activity. Unbelievable.

So the moral of the story is, do not give up if you are diagnosed. If they've caught it in time, you will be a survivor as I have been and am today. If they're able to offer you surgery, chemo and/or radiotherapy, they would not do so unless they were convinced the cancer was treatable. If it is treatable and you haven't been given a life sentence, you have every chance of surviving.

Positive Mental Attitude is very important when undergoing cancer, so when you feel strong and not tired, you have to get out and do what you want to do. I used to shop and clean in the mornings, see friends for lunch and then rest in the afternoon. Give in to the tiredness, and sleep or rest when you are tired. It allows your body time to recover.

Wear makeup, do your hair, get dressed and don't hide. Then you will not only look normal but will feel normal. You do not want to look or feel like a cancer patient. It is very easy to give in and not fight. Somehow, somewhere you will find the inner strength to do all of these things and continue your life.

Living with cancer has changed my perspective on life. I now live for today, as do my family. We no longer book holidays in advance as we don't want to risk cancelling them. We appreciate every day that we have together as no-one knows what is round the corner. We never take each other for granted, and indeed, this life changing experience has bonded us closer together as a family. You find out who your true friends are, who stands by you through thick and thin. You realise how lucky you are.

Do not look on cancer as the end. It is not always the end. Look upon it as a challenge and a fight to survive it. You can do it. If you're aware of any changes in your body, get them checked out immediately. Just a simple x-ray or blood test can tell you so much. Don't be afraid or scared to investigate as this can save your life.

I have survived cancer four times now and think that is more than enough of my fair share. I do believe, however, that I have had to undergo this to help others.

Awareness is important and, if acted upon quickly, will save your life. Never, ever give up. Life is so precious - make the most of it and enjoy it. Never take things for granted; instead cherish the important moments. Enjoy life for your family and friends, but most of all, enjoy it for you. You can survive, no matter what, if you believe you are indestructible and if you have a purpose.

I do sound like I am lecturing, but you know what, having lived through the unliveable shows there is a reason to be here, and that is to share my experience with you. If I can help just one person cope. You can do it for you or others you know and love. You can be respected for your determination to enjoy every moment, get through it all and live life with more compassion, understanding and gratitude.

Acknowledgements

This book is dedicated to my late mother Hilary Adler
Also in loving Memory of my late mother-in-law Coralie Brenner

Thanks to my loving husband, Russell Brenner
My Wonderful Son, Marc Brenner
My Dad, Maurice Adler
Our gorgeous dog, Bentley
My Brother in laws, Clifford & Warwick Brenner
My Sister in laws, Rachel & Debra Brenner
Nieces & Nephews, Harley, Coco, Oliver, Kane & Rocco Brenner
Cousin Sue, Mel and Millie

Thanks to:
Andrew Olins
Andrea & Ashley Rubin
Helen Rollason Cancer Charity
St Clare Hospice
Isabel Hospice
Rivers Hospital Complex including the Gardens Neuro Centre

Special Donations from:
Dudrich (Holdings) Ltd & Studio 434
Harwoods Ltd
Hills of Woodford
P&A Wood
Tangent International Ltd

Thank you to everyone that has purchased this book in memory of Lisa.